Badgers
in the Dark

By Sofia Maximus

Gareth Stevens
Publishing

Please visit our website, www.garethstevens.com. For a free color catalog of all our high-quality books, call toll free 1-800-542-2595 or fax 1-877-542-2596.

Library of Congress Cataloging-in-Publication Data

Maximus, Sofia.
Badgers in the dark / Sofia Maximus.
    p. cm. — (Creatures of the night)
Includes index.
ISBN 978-1-4339-6362-9 (pbk.)
ISBN 978-1-4339-6363-6 (6-pack)
ISBN 978-1-4339-6480-0 (library binding)
1. Badgers—Juvenile literature. 2. Nocturnal animals—Juvenile literature. I. Title.
QL737.C25M326 2012
599.76'7—dc23

                                        2011018387

First Edition

Published in 2013 by
Gareth Stevens Publishing
111 East 14th Street, Suite 349
New York, NY 10003

Copyright © 2013 Gareth Stevens Publishing

Designer: Daniel Hosek
Editor: Therese Shea

Photo credits: Cover, pp. 1, 21 iStockphoto.com/Thinkstock.com; pp. 5, 17, 19, 20 Shutterstock.com; p. 7 John E. Marriott/Getty Images; p. 9 Laurie Campbell/Stone/Getty Images; p. 11 Tom Brakefield/ Photodisc/Getty Images; p. 13 David Tipling/Photographer's Choice/Getty Images; p. 15 Robert Harding Images/Masterfile.com.

Printed in the United States of America

CPSIA compliance information: Batch #CW12GS: For further information contact Gareth Stevens, New York, New York at 1-800-542-2595.

Contents

Meet the Badger 4

Super Diggers! 6

Night Hunters 12

Baby Badgers 14

Sleepy Winter 16

Two Kinds of Badgers 18

Glossary 22

For More Information 23

Index 24

Boldface words appear in the glossary.

Meet the Badger

What has a black-and-white face, long claws, and comes out at night? A badger! A badger is a medium-size animal with short legs and a short, bushy tail. It has a white stripe from its nose to its shoulders or even further.

5

Super Diggers!

Badgers are famous for their digging. They dig to find food. Badgers eat animals they find underground, such as ground squirrels and **prairie dogs**. They also eat rabbits, **rodents**, lizards, birds, and bugs.

Badgers dig homes under the ground. These are called **burrows**. A burrow may be deep. It may have many rooms joined by tunnels. A badger digs a large room to sleep in. Some kinds of badgers dig many burrows.

Badgers dig to hide. They can dig fast to escape danger. If they can't hide, badgers fight. They use their sharp claws and teeth. Badgers don't have many enemies in nature, though. People are their greatest enemy.

11

Night Hunters

Badgers mostly come out at night. They're **nocturnal**. The dark helps them hide while they look for food. Badgers have good senses of smell, sight, and hearing. These help them hunt in the dark.

13

Baby Badgers

Badgers are **mammals**. Mother badgers have one to five babies each year. The babies are blind at first. The mother feeds them for several months. Young badgers leave their mother after about 6 months.

Sleepy Winter

Badgers like to sleep through the cold months of winter. Their burrows are much warmer than the outside air. However, badgers wake up easily in winter. Sometimes, they go out to hunt on warm winter days.

17

Two Kinds of Badgers

There are two kinds of badgers. The American badger lives in Canada, the United States, and Mexico. It's mostly gray or reddish and has a yellowish belly. It likes to live alone in an area with few trees.

The European badger lives in Europe and northern Asia. It's mostly gray with black arms, legs, and belly. It's larger than the American badger. European badgers like to live in groups of up to 12 badgers.

European

The Badger Fact Box

Kind	Length	Weight
American badger	20 to 35 inches (51 to 89 cm)	8 to 25 pounds (4 to 11 kg)
European badger	27 to 43 inches (69 to 109 cm)	22 to 44 pounds (10 to 20 kg)

Glossary

burrow: a hole or tunnel dug as a living space by an animal

mammal: an animal that has live young and feeds them milk from the mother's body

nocturnal: active at night

prairie dog: a small animal in the squirrel family that lives underground

rodent: a small animal with large teeth, such as a mouse or rat

For More Information

Books

Leach, Michael. *Badger*. New York, NY: PowerKids Press, 2009.

Solway, Andrew. *Killer Carnivores*. Chicago, IL: Heinemann Library, 2005.

Websites

American Badger
animaldiversity.ummz.umich.edu/site/accounts/information/Taxidea_taxus.html
See photos of the American badger as well as its burrow.

Do You Want to Be a Badger?
www.dnr.state.wi.us/eek/critter/mammal/badger.htm
Learn more about badgers and how they act.

Index

American badger 18, 20, 21

babies 14

birds 6

black-and-white face 4

bugs 6

burrows 8, 16

Canada 18

claws 4, 10

digging 6, 8, 10

enemies 10

European badger 20, 21

fight 10

food 6, 12

ground squirrels 6

hunt 12, 16

legs 4, 20

lizards 6

mammals 14

Mexico 18

nocturnal 12

prairie dogs 6

rabbits 6

rodents 6

senses 12

sleep 8, 16

stripe 4

tail 4

teeth 10

United States 18

winter 16